PRESENTED TO:

_____

FROM:

_____

ON THE OCCASION OF:

_____

The 12 WAYS of CHRISTMAS

DAVID JEREMIAH

THOMAS NELSON
Since 1798

NASHVILLE   DALLAS   MEXICO CITY   RIO DE JANEIRO   BEIJING

The 12 Ways of Christmas
© 2008 by David Jeremiah

Published in Nashville, Tennessee, by Thomas Nelson. Thomas Nelson is a registered trademark of Thomas Nelson, Inc.

Published in association with Yates & Yates, LLP, Attorneys and Literary Agents, Orange, CA

Special thanks to Robert J. Morgan and William Kruidenier for assistance in writing *The 12 Ways of Christmas*.

All rights reserved. No portion of this publication may be reproduced, stored in a retrieval system, or transmitted by any means—electronic, mechanical, photocopying, recording, or any other—except for brief quotations in printed reviews, without the prior written permission of the publisher.

Thomas Nelson, Inc. titles may be purchased in bulk for educational, business, fund-raising, or sales promotional use. For information, please e-mail SpecialMarkets@ThomasNelson.com.

Unless otherwise noted, Scripture references are from THE NEW KING JAMES VERSION. © 1982 by Thomas Nelson, Inc. Used by permission. All rights reserved.

Scripture quotations marked HCSB are taken from the HOLMAN CHRISTIAN STANDARD BIBLE. © 1999, 2000, 2002, 2003 by Broadman and Holman Publishers. All rights reserved.

Scripture quotations marked NET are taken from the NEW ENGLISH TRANSLATION. © 1996-2007 by Biblical Studies Press (BSP), L.L.C. and authors. All rights reserved.

Scripture quotations marked KJV are taken from The Holy Bible, KING JAMES VERSION.

Creative Editor: Paul Joiner
Content Editor: Cathy Lord
Project Manager: Lisa Stilwell
Designed by: DesignWorks Group, Sisters, Oregon

ISBN-10: 1-4041-8727-8
ISBN-13: 978-1-4041-8727-6

Printed and bound in China

www.thomasnelson.com

09 10 11 12—9 8 7 6 5 4 3 2

TABLE OF CONTENTS

WONDER

If you engage a typical American child below the age of, say, eight, and ask him what he would most like to know about Christmas, you might get an answer along these lines: "I wonder how Santa Claus carries enough toys in his sleigh for all the kids in the world." "I wonder how Santa gets in my house since we don't have a chimney." "I wonder how reindeer can fly." "I wonder why nobody's ever seen Santa's house at the North Pole."

In other words, the sense of wonder children have about Christmas is all about Santa Claus, not Jesus! When the true meaning of Christmas is understood, here are some things I've heard children wonder about: "Where did Jesus live before He came to live on earth?" "How could God become a baby?" "What did the baby Jesus come to earth to do?" "Why was Jesus born in a stable with animals instead of in a hospital?"

Those are good questions, whether asked by a child or an adult! Those questions (and some more that are even deeper) represent the sense of wonder that ought to resurface in our minds at this time of year. Yet, too often, we find ourselves so caught up in the busyness of Christmas that we don't take time to reflect on the wonderment of it all.

The first Christmas was certainly surrounded by wonder:

· Zacharias wondered how he and his elderly wife could give birth to the forerunner of the Messiah (*Luke 1:18*).

· Mary wondered how it would be possible for a virgin to give birth to a baby (*Luke 1:34*).

· Joseph wondered why he and Mary had been chosen by God to be the parents of the Messiah (*Matthew 1:18—25*).

· The shepherds in the fields outside Bethlehem wondered about the angels that appeared in the sky, and what their message meant (*Luke 2:13—15*).

· Those in Bethlehem wondered about the story that the shepherds were spreading throughout the village (*Luke 2:17—18*).

· Mary wondered about everything that was happening at the birth of her baby (*Luke 2:19*).

· Simeon wondered at the blessing of being able, before he died, to see the child-Messiah (*Luke 2:25–32*).

· Mary and Joseph "marveled" at the words prophesied by Simeon about their baby, Jesus (*Luke 2:33–35*).

· People in the temple that day no doubt wondered about the words of the prophetess Anna, who spoke about the redemption to come through the baby Jesus (*Luke 2:36–38*).

· The Magi must have wondered about the meaning of the star they saw, and the baby to whom they brought gifts, and about the dream that warned them against Herod (*Matthew 2:1–12*).

· Joseph wondered about his dream that warned him to take Mary and Jesus and flee to Egypt to avoid Herod (*Matthew 2:13–15*).

Those are just the moments of wonder that are recorded for us in Scripture. But think how many more countless moments there must have been among the people of Nazareth and Judea who were witnesses to the first Christmas: A virgin conceiving a child? Angels in the sky? The Messiah born in a stable, sleeping in a manger? Royal officials from the east appearing and worshiping this baby? Prophets in the temple declaring that Jesus was the Messiah, never having seen Him before? King Herod killing scores of male babies? What did it all mean?

What would you and I have thought if we had been living there when the first Christmas took place? How many nights would we have sat up late talking about these events, trying to put two and two together? I can assure you we would have exhibited far more wonder than we do today.

Today at Christmas, people tend to wonder about a whole different set of events:

· I wonder if we should get Bobby the new iPhone now or wait for the second generation to come out? Maybe it'll be cheaper then and have more features.

· I wonder if we should fly to Mom and Dad's place this Christmas, or bring them here? Are they getting too old for the hassles of flying? Maybe that's asking too much of them.

· I wonder if we should set limits on our gift buying this year? You know we didn't get last year's credit card bills paid until this past June.

· I wonder what ever happened to the way Christmas used to be? You know, sitting by the fire, Christmas carols, simple gifts. I wonder if we could ever get that back?

That last bit of wondering is a valuable one. A good place to start this year is to spend some time reflecting on the wonders of the true Christmas story. Raise the questions, study the Scriptures, give thanks for what you know, and pray about what you don't.

Wondering and marveling at what God has done. It's one of the twelve ways of Christmas.

SACRIFICE

Jim and Della were young, starting their marriage with nothing and getting by on little more. Eight dollars a week for a flat took a big bite out of Jim's twenty-dollar-a-week salary. But what they lacked in material things, they made up for with love.

Christmas came and Della despaired over the $1.87 (60 cents of it in pennies) she had been able to save for Jim's Christmas present—until she looked in the mirror and saw the one thing she had that was worth something: her beautiful knee-length hair. Jim loved her long hair, but it would grow back. And with the money she could buy Jim a gold chain for his most valued possession—the watch he had inherited from his grandfather, then his father. With the $20 in hand she got for her hair, she bought the gold chain and waited anxiously for Jim to get home from work.

His crestfallen face at the sight of Della's short hair was not for the reason she thought. He professed his love for her regardless of the length of her hair, then handed Della his gift for her: a set of tortoiseshell combs with jeweled edges for Della to wear in her now-gone hair—bought with the money he got for his heirloom gold watch. Two young lovers sacrificed all they had for the sake of their beloved's joy at Christmas.

O. Henry's short story *The Gift of the Magi* has become a Christmas classic because it reveals the heart of the Christmas story: sacrificial love. The author himself concluded his story this way: "But in a last word to the wise of these days, let it be said that of all who give gifts, these two were the wisest. Of all who give and receive gifts, such as they are wisest." [1]

Why? Because Della and Jim discovered that love and sacrifice are synonyms, that the deeper the cost of giving, the deeper the experience of love and joy.

Sacrifice, of course, is what the true Christmas story is all about. It is not so much about giving as it is about sacrificing. (All sacrifice is

22

giving, but not all giving is sacrifice.) Even if God had more than one Son to give up for the sake of His sin-stained creation, to give even one would have been a sacrifice. But to send His only Son from the glory of heaven to the grind of earth, knowing what would befall Him while He was here—that's sacrifice.

Sacrifice means to give to another person something we could have kept for ourselves. It means to choose, to deny, to love, to give, and to find the deepest pleasure in another's joy. Because the heart of the Christmas message is sacrifice, we ought to look for ways this year to give sacrificially. That doesn't necessarily mean emptying your bank account for the poor out of a guilt complex. It means to look for ways to put others' needs, desires, and joy ahead of our own.

It was the nineteenth-century Protestant clergyman Henry Ward Beecher who said, "In this world, it is not what we take up, but what

23

we give up, that makes us rich."[2] In that sense, there are lots of ways to "become rich" at Christmas. We can set aside money all year long that we might have spent on ourselves and use it to bless others with a gift. We can sacrifice our time and our money to reach out to those for whom Christmas may not be a joyous time of the year: the homeless, students who aren't able to travel home for the holiday, shut-ins, those in hospitals, prisons, and shelters—and don't overlook the elderly neighbor who lives alone or who might be experiencing the first Christmas after the death of a spouse.

There is no shortage of opportunities to sacrifice. All we have to do is look for the need. That's what God did when He sent His Son into the world at the first Christmas. The need was twofold: for the human race to see what had been lost in the Garden of Eden—perfect humanity; and to restore what was lost—fellowship with God through the forgiveness of sins. Once the need is identified, the gift becomes obvious.

The challenge is to be willing to provide a gift as big as the need. Sometimes the need is bigger than what we can comfortably give in terms of time or treasure. And that's where sacrifice comes in. Giving becomes sacrificial when we take something we might normally have channeled toward ourselves and dedicate it to increasing the joy of another.

The way of sacrifice is the way of the One who said, *"It is more blessed to give than to receive"* (Acts 20:35).

HUMILITY

Have you ever celebrated a holiday named *Memas*?

Some people observe it every December 25. For them, the *Christ* of Christmas has been replaced by a me-centered worldview. This is a celebrity generation in which everyone wants little flashes of fame and fortune. One of the reasons the average wedding costs almost thirty thousand dollars is because so many couples want to experience for at least a day the kind of endless glamour enjoyed by celebs.

Even Christmas has been affected; and if we aren't careful, it becomes all about *us*—our schedules, our diets, our budgets, our wish lists, our time off, our vacation, our parking spaces, our gifts to enjoy or return.

I love the trappings of Christmas as much as anyone; but the *truths* of Christmas trump the *trappings* of Christmas, and too many people get trapped in the trappings and forget the truth. How can we enjoy

Christmas if *we're* the reason for the season?

In a sense, of course, Christmas is all about us. God loved *us*, became flesh for *us*, died to forgive *us* our sins, and rose to give *us* everlasting life. Christmas is the celebration of what Jesus did for us. But in return, we should make it all about Him: loving *Him*, serving *Him*, praising *Him*, and emulating His attitude of humility.

29

Here are three words to remember during December. You might write them on a piece of paper to keep in your pocket or purse through the holidays.

PATIENCE

I don't know about you, but I'm tempted with impatience more in December than any other time. As our schedules accelerate, our emotions are drained like gasoline in an SUV. We fly from event to event, battle crowds at the shopping centers, endure delays at the airports, run back and forth to church, and have family members invading our houses. Sometimes all it takes is a momentary flash of anger or an irritable expression on our faces—and we've ruined someone's day.

Dr. F. B. Meyer told of a schoolteacher who, when provoked by a group of unruly kids, prayed: "Your patience, Lord!" [3] Instantly such

a calm entered him that he realized he had made a great discovery. It's not enough to tell ourselves to be patient, or even to ask God for patience. We need to claim His very own patience and appropriate His own indwelling resources at the very moment of irritation.

SACRIFICE

A word that isn't mentioned in many of our carols is *sacrifice*. Jesus didn't just give eternal life, wonderful as that is. He gave us *Himself*. He died sacrificially for the sins of the world, and He rose to live on our behalf.

A natural question arises from His sacrifice: In what way can I sacrifice something of myself for someone else this season? I'm not going to suggest any answers for you, but I'm mulling it over for me. All service requires sacrifice, and we shouldn't offer the Lord that which costs us nothing.

33

OTHERS

The third word is *others*. Remember the old acronym for joy—Jesus first, others second, yourself last? There are two kinds of people in the world—those who come into a room saying, "Here I am!" And others who enter a room saying, "Ah, there you are!"

This season, build up others and make them feel special—and not just people at home or church. What about that woman at the shopping mall who might need a parking space more than you do? What about the harried clerk at the discount store who could use a smile? What about the man in line behind you?

Patience, sacrifice, and joy—that's the way to display humility, and that's the way to celebrate *Christ*mas instead of *Me*mas.

CHARITY

The word *charity* became most famous in the English language by its use in the King James Version of the Bible, especially in Paul's chapter on love *(1 Corinthians 13)*. But it has suffered some disuse as the word *love* has replaced it in modern translations. Today, *charity* is a catch-all term to describe nonprofit organizations that help the poor and needy.

But *charity* is a good word—a strong, proactive word. Its roots are in the Latin words for *affection* ("caritas") and *dear* ("carus"). It's not best used to describe an organization (a charity), but to describe an action—a charitable act or gesture, motivated by genuine affection and caring.

Since 1950, the word *charity* has been personified by the actions of the Missionaries of Charity, which began with twelve workers in

Calcutta. Today there are forty-five hundred workers all over the world continuing the work of Mother Teresa. And what was her work? In her own words, it was to care for (extend charity to) "the hungry, the naked, the homeless, the crippled, the blind, the lepers, all those people who feel unwanted, unloved, uncared for throughout society, people that have become a burden to the society and are shunned by everyone."[4]

39

We are all challenged by Mother Teresa and the Missionaries of Charity, and we have to admire their willingness to go *looking* for ways to extend the love of God. They don't sit back and wait for the needy to come to them. They go out into the streets of the world's largest cities and find those who have been "shunned by everyone"—and bring them in and meet their needs. That is the true heart of charity—of love. God didn't wait for the human race to come to Him for help. He sent forth His own Son into the world to seek out and save that which was lost *(Luke 19:10)*. God's charity—His *agape* love—was the reason for the first Christmas.

At that first Christmas, there was a young couple who had been "shunned by everyone." They had journeyed for days to get to Bethlehem, although Mary's baby was due at any moment. Bethlehem was a small village to begin with, and had been swollen by others like

Mary and Joseph who had traveled to the village of their forefather, David, to register for the Roman census. There, in the streets filled with all of Joseph's cousins, they wondered where they would find a place for Mary to rest—and probably deliver her baby.

Luke is precise in his language when he says there was no room for them *"in the inn" (Luke 2:7)*. The suggestion is that Bethlehem had only one inn where travelers might stay the night, and it was full when Mary and Joseph arrived. Perhaps they had looked all over town for a place to stay . . . perhaps they pleaded with the innkeeper for something, anything . . . perhaps the innkeeper saw Mary's bulging robes, her stooped posture, her hand on her stomach.

Whatever the reason, the innkeeper helped the young couple who would soon become parents. He led them to the stable, perhaps the

place where guests at the inn kept their animals, and helped arrange
a place for Mary to rest. It wasn't much, but it was a roof and dry
straw—and a manger (a feeding trough for the animals), should
Mary deliver the baby that night. It wasn't much, but the innkeeper
did what he could.

Jesus' story of the "good Samaritan" is as good a human illustration
of charity as we will ever find *(Luke 10:30–37)*. Before the Samaritan
encountered the man who had been attacked, robbed, and left for
dead, two others had passed by and done nothing. But the Samaritan
crossed the road and extended love and compassion; he bandaged the
man and took him to an inn and paid for his room and board while
he recovered. He couldn't do everything, but he did what he could.
And Jesus concluded the story by saying, "Go and do likewise."

44

All around us at Christmas this year there will be those less fortunate than we are. We can pass by on the other side of the road, or we can cross over and do what we can to make their life, and their Christmas, more comfortable. Charity toward others is affection and caring based on the active response of Christ to our needs. Giving money to charities is commendable—there are many that do good works. But don't pass up the opportunities God gives you this Christmas to personally "be charitable" to others.

Extending a helping hand to those in need—being charitable—is one of the ways of Christmas.

CREATIVITY

One recent Christmas, the British village of Barrow wanted a "real live hero" to switch on the Christmas lights in the town square. After looking high and low, they found their hero—a three-year-old boy named Jake who had battled cancer twice, undergone chemotherapy thirteen times, and spent his first two Christmases in the hospital. That night, Jake rode a chauffeur-driven limousine to the square where, amid cheers, he lit up the tree for the whole town to enjoy. [5]

It took some creativity to choose a three-year-old as town hero, but how appropriate! Jesus was small and tiny, just a child; yet He turned on the Christmas lights for all the world.

Creativity is the hallmark of Christmas. Think of the originality that went into the first Christmas. Every feature was a surprise, for nothing seemed to follow the natural scheme of things. The eternal God in a manger. No room in the inn. Visitors on camels. Shepherds in their fields. The star. No one but the Creator Himself would have scripted it that way.

49

I love Christmas *traditions*, but traditions are simply innovations that have been around awhile. Any tradition can become stale, given enough time. We need to keep our customs original with little moments of different-ness, and we need to keep inventing "new traditions" by finding fresh ways of honoring Christ.

ASK YOURSELF

Ask yourself, "What can I do differently this year?" We're seldom
creative on the spot. We have to mull things over and think things
through. Take some quiet walks and ask yourself how to keep
Christmas fresh in your heart and family. As you come up with
ideas, it may change the way you shop, the food you cook, the
money you spend, the places you go, and even the songs you sing.
One church, having sung Christmas carols for several weeks, chose
no carols on Christmas Sunday. Instead, the worship leader selected
non-Christmas hymns about Jesus, such as "Fairest Lord Jesus."
The congregation had a different (but worshipful) feel that day
while singing, "O Thou of God and man the Son! Thee will I
cherish, Thee will I honor. . . ."

51

ASK YOUR FAMILY

Ask your family, "What can we do differently this year?" I know one couple who, early in their marriage, were invited by friends to brunch. It was a fabulous spread—sausage-and-egg casserole, fruit salad, chicken roll-ups, bran muffins, fresh juice. My friends asked for the recipes, and that menu became their annual Christmas Brunch, the only time all year when they prepare that particular feast. The basic dishes never change; but every year, they try new side items so that it's always old, yet ever new.

If you ask your youngsters about decorating the house for Christmas, they'll probably come up with things you've never thought of; and some of the ideas might be good! If you ask your friends how they'd like to exchange gifts, you might be surprised at the answers.

ASK GOD

Truly creative people derive their creativity from the Creator, so it's important to ask God how He'd have you celebrate Christmas. He alone can create out of nothing. We're only creative in a secondary sense, taking what He has already made and "fiddling" with it. Ask Him to show you fresh and meaningful ways to celebrate Jesus in your heart, in your family, and in your church.

55

If a three-year-old can become a town's hero, and if a Babe in the manger can be the world's Savior, we can rise above our traditions and enjoy Christmas again this year, as though for the first time. This is a season for surprises, so bring out of your storehouse treasures both old and new (*Matthew 13:52*).

This is the way of Christmas.

SIMPLICITY

In 1926, the Neiman Marcus Company started publishing an annual catalog of unusual Christmas gifts; but for a number of years, the publication attracted little attention. Then in 1959, the Marcus brothers decided to generate publicity with eye-popping gifts for the "person who has everything." That year they offered a Black Angus steer, to be delivered either on the hoof or in steaks with a silver-plated outdoor cooker. Each year since, the gifts have become more extravagant. Last year's catalog included a $1.44 million special edition Gem Triton submarine, with a gemstone keychain. If that's too pricey for you there are his and hers portraits in chocolate syrup for a mere $110,000. [6]

59

But Christmas can get out of hand even if you aren't a Neiman Marcus fan. The stress and strain on our schedules and budgets isn't what God intends; and I want to humbly suggest that if the holidays leave you worse for wear, you need to heed Henry David Thoreau's famous dictum: "Simplify! Simplify!"

· Set a spending cap for yourself, and covenant not to spend more than a certain amount for any one gift, no matter how "perfect" it is.

· Reduce your gift list. Even one less person can be a significant savings of time, money, and energy.

· Cut back on your schedule. You don't have to attend every party or accept every invitation. Sit down with your December calendar and reserve some evenings for peace and quiet. (The secret words are: "I'm sorry; my schedule won't allow it.")

· Don't worry if your decorations aren't all up. Less is more. You can vary from year to year which ones to use.

· Take time for your devotions during the season. Keep a journal of your daily Bible reading, and select thirty-one people during the month to receive a special gift of prayer. You might compose a special prayer for each one, jot it on a Christmas card, and tell them it's your heartfelt gift for them this season.

Remember, it's possible to slow down when we have to. If you're clipping along at seventy miles per hour on the freeway and come to a construction zone, you have to slow down whether you like it or not. If you're working seventy hours a week and come down with the flu, you have to slow down long enough to recover.

How much better to slow down by choice! Manage the season instead of letting it manage you. We can't do it all, so we have to tackle the important things and leave the rest in God's hands. It's His agenda we should fulfill, and His burdens are light.

In the Dick Francis novel *Under Orders*, the main character, Sid Halley, meets a political friend inside the complex of the British Parliament Building in London. Here's the way he put it:

> *I arrived at the Peers' Entrance at one o'clock exactly . . . . The tones of Big Ben were still ringing in my ears as I stepped into the revolving door, a time-warp portal rotating me from the hustle and bustle of twenty-first-century London on the outside to the sedate world of nineteenth-century quiet and formality on the inside. . . .* [7]

We all need a portal through which we can find a quieter life, at least occasionally. For too many of us, Christmas is a nightmarish revolving door in which we're spinning faster and faster. But the wiser among us find it a sort of time-warp portal, rotating us from the hustle and bustle of twenty-first-century life to the sedate world of a quieter time.

So this year, slow down, look up, breathe deeply, spend less—and simplify, simplify! The way of a calmed Christmas—simplicity.

AFFECTION

When Katie Fisher was seventeen years old, she experienced one of
the ways of Christmas from a group of complete strangers. Katie had
been battling Burkitt's lymphoma, a fast-growing malignancy, since
February—months of hospitalization, numerous rounds of chemotherapy, and unrelenting pain. She had taken one of her lambs to the
local Junior Livestock Sale in hopes of raising some spending money.

When the lamb came up for auction, the auctioneer let folks
in the arena know about Katie's situation anticipating that her
lamb would bring a bit more than the $2 per pound average. And
did it ever! The lamb sold for $11.50 per pound—but then the
buyer gave it back so it could be sold again. Every time it would
sell, a cry of "Re-sell!" would be heard and the lamb would be
sold again. Families and businesses bought and sold Katie's lamb
thirty-six times, netting her more than $16,000 that went to

help pay for her medical expenses. And the last buyer gave Katie back her lamb to keep for good.[8]

What is it that rises up in the human heart and moves people to give toward a child in need? Compassion? Yes. Love? Definitely. Empathy? Often. Let's gather all those virtues and emotions together and call them affection—one of the ways of Christmas.

71

The dictionary says that *affection* is a "tender feeling toward another; a disposition to feel, do, or say." We normally think of affection as being toward a person we know well, toward whom we show affection with a hug or a kiss. Affection toward loved ones is certainly appropriate. But it is not only toward those we know well that we can "feel tender" or be "disposed to feel, do, or say" kind things.

David, the king of Israel, directed his affection toward the temple, and demonstrated it by giving sacrificially toward its construction (*1 Chronicles 29:3*). Paul encouraged Christians to be "kindly affectionate" to every member of the church (*Romans 12:10*). Paul also felt great affection for the Christians in Philippi (*Philippians 1:8*)

and expected them to be affectionate toward one another *(2:1–2)*. And by all means, husbands are expected to be affectionate toward their wives *(1 Corinthians 7:3)*.

So affection is appropriate in a wide range of situations. But, like unconditional love, affection can be a challenge in some circumstances. Consider the affection Joseph was expected to demonstrate toward his fiancée, Mary. He was engaged to her when he discovered she was pregnant. Even though, by Jewish law, he would have been justified in making a public issue out of her apparent infidelity *(Deuteronomy 22:23–24)*, he chose what was best for her—returning her quietly to her parents *(Matthew 1:19)*.

That step would have been a challenge to Joseph's affections, no doubt. But then he was challenged again when God revealed to him that Mary's pregnancy was by the Holy Spirit, that she had remained pure and righteous, and that Joseph should remain married to her and become the father to her child. While Joseph was sorting out this deluge of information and feelings, his affection for Mary won the day. It was no doubt a difficult situation, having to weather the stares and gossip from those who didn't—who couldn't—understand what was going on.

This Christmas, you will be around lots of different people: family and loved ones, acquaintances, strangers, and others. Toward some, your affection will be generous and easy. For those, don't take their closeness for granted—be lovingly affectionate at this special time of the year. But for others, your affection may be a challenge. Perhaps they are

people you don't know well. Or perhaps they are some you know all too well—some with whom you are brought together by the holiday social scene. May I encourage you to be kindly affectionate to them? Like love, affection must be unconditional if it is to be real, the same way God's affection and love are toward us. Conditional affection may go unexpressed because the conditions are unmet. If it is expressed, it will likely be formal and stiff at best and hypocritical at worst.

When you read the story of Katie Fisher and her repeatedly-sold lamb, if you thought, *I would have bid on that lamb to help a suffering teenager*, then you have what affection requires: a tender spirit toward others and a predisposition to reach out with love and comfort. This Christmas, show your affection to all. A gift, an embrace, a letter, a helping hand, a visit, a kind word—not to mention an act of reconciliation or forgiveness where needed—will go a long way toward making this Christmas a most loving one.

Affection—a way of Christmas that brings givers and receivers together in new and tender ways.

REFLECTION

I've never looked so out of shape—fat, bloated, heavy in the middle, legs like tree stumps, arms like sewer pipes. The next minute, I faced an opposite set of problems: I looked like a ten-foot pole with big feet. My kids laughed, and we all had fun in the hall of mirrors at the county fair. The thin, flexible mirrors, called distortion mirrors,

were curved, twisted, and bent so as to warp the images and reflect a distorted sense of reality.

If you want to see real distortion, aim the mirror of our popular culture at the Christmas story in the Gospels. The "holidays" no longer reflect the true meaning of Christmas. John MacArthur, in

81

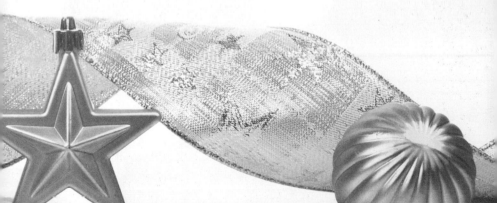

82

his *Incarnation of the Triune God*, wrote, "Christmas has really become a hopeless muddle of confusion. The humility and the poverty of the stable are somehow confused with the wealth and indulgence and selfishness of gift giving. The quietness of Bethlehem is mingled with the din of shopping malls and freeway traffic. The soberness of the Incarnation is somehow mixed with the drunkenness of this season." [9]

83

The paradox of Christmas is heard in the sounds—the honking of car horns, the jingling of bells, the laughing of children, the strains of the carolers, the "Ho, ho, ho" of department store Santas; it's all a part of the frenzy of the season. Yet the best Christmas moments are the quiet ones, and the best reflection of Christmas takes place in the mirror of our own hearts.

One verse in the Bible tells us exactly how to celebrate Christmas, and who better than Mary herself to set the example? *Luke 2:19 says, "But Mary kept all these things and pondered them in her heart."*

Pondering is a word worth pondering. According to the dictionary, it means "to weigh in the mind, to think about, to reflect on." This describes a biblical pattern, for the Psalmist wrote: *"Reflect in your heart and be still. . . . I will reflect on all You have done and meditate on Your actions. . . . I reflect on the work of Your hands" (Psalm 4:4; 77:12; 143:5, HCSB).*

"Sober reflection is good for the heart," says Ecclesiastes 7:3 (NET).

There are lots of ways to practice the art of personal reflection during the holidays. The final moments of the day are often the best when the kids are in bed and we walk through the house a final time to

turn off the lights and lock the doors. In the darkness with only the twinkling glow of the Christmas tree lights, it's fun to sink into a chair, hand curled around a cup of cocoa, and ponder the ageless wonders of Christmas.

It's also wonderful to gather the family around the tree for a traditional reading of the Christmas story, perhaps on Christmas Eve. I grew up hearing the Christmas story told in the classic language of the old King James Version, and to me it's still beautiful: *"And it came to pass in those days, that there went out a decree from Caesar Augustus that all the world should be taxed . . ." (Luke 2:1).* Reading those words to my grandchildren can still bring a tear to my eyes.

87

How wonderful to arrive early for Christmas Eve services and sit quietly in the pew listening to the strains of the organ, or relax at our desk as a candle flickers in the darkness, or get up early on Christmas Day to watch the sunrise glow in the east. How wonderful to reflect on the timeless story of Jesus, keeping it in mind and pondering these things in your heart.

It's one of the best ways of Christmas.

GIVING

We would be less than honest if we didn't admit it: Christmas in America is all about gifts. Or, perhaps we should say, all about shopping and *mostly* about gifts for others. The increase in the commercialization of Christmas is astonishing for those of us who've been around a few decades. Just when we think Christmas couldn't possibly be made more commercial, the retailers and advertisers figure out a way to do it. A large percentage of the average retailer's revenue is generated in November and December of each year—it's the pot of gold at the end of their retailing rainbow.

In 2006, the National Retail Federation estimated that holiday sales would total $457.4 billion and 2007 spending patterns were very similar. Their survey of 7,623 shoppers (prior to the start of the November 1–December 31 season) revealed that shoppers would spend an average of:

- $451.34 on family.
- $85.60 on friends.
- $22.40 on coworkers.
- $44.52 on acquaintances such as teachers, clergy, babysitters, and others.
- And $99.22 on themselves, prompted by holiday discounts [10] (That's why I said Christmas is *mostly* about gifts for others. It almost looks like buying gifts for others is a way to justify spending money on one's self.)

Interestingly, convenience seems to play a significant part in holiday gift giving. More than $29 billion of the 2007 shopping total was spent online, and $35 billion was spent on gift cards. Just imagine how much easier it would have been for the Magi if they could have purchased their gold, frankincense, and myrrh over the Internet and had them delivered directly to Bethlehem. It would have saved them several months' worth of saddle sores, not to mention a life-threatening encounter with a vindictive king named Herod. Or, if they weren't sure that gold and precious spices were the right gifts for the newborn King, they could have just purchased gift cards and let Mary pick out something that Jesus needed.

That fanciful scenario suggests just how far we have come from the humble actions of several ancient "wise men" who established the pattern of gift giving at the first Christmas. They spared no expense in their gifts of gold, frankincense, and myrrh. They gave their gifts humbly. They gave their gifts personally. They gave their gifts thoughtfully—royal gifts for a newborn King. The way the Magi gave their gifts should serve as a model for how we give.

I don't mean we have to give as expensively as they did or deliver all our gifts in person. And there's certainly nothing wrong with shopping online or giving a gift card. If I had to choose a word to summarize Christian Christmas gift giving, I think I would choose *appreciatively*. If we give gifts to one another appreciatively, we'll be saying, "I honor and appreciate you. I've selected this gift for you because I want you to know how much I value you and the role you play in my life. This gift isn't a payment—it's an expression of what I could never repay or replace: your unique friendship."

Isn't that what the very first Christmas gift represented to those who received it? No, I'm not talking about the Magi's gifts to the baby Jesus. I'm talking about the gift of Jesus Himself to you and me. Jesus once referred to His coming into the world as *"the gift of God"* (John 4:10), and Paul also referred to our eternal life as *"the gift of God"* (Romans 6:23). And the apostle John talked about all who received the gift of God gaining the *"right to become children of God"* (John 1:12).

So Jesus' entry into the world was indeed the first Christmas gift. God gave something of infinite value to say to us, "I love you more than you can imagine. I want you to know how valuable you are to Me." Our gifts to one another at Christmas ought to be a reflection of God's first gift to us. When we give to others, it ought to be an expression of gratitude for what God has given to us. The generosity and appreciation revealed through our gifts ought to say to the recipient, "Everything I know about giving I learned from God's gift of Jesus Christ to me."

Is that too idealistic? Perhaps. But remember that maturity is our goal in all the Christian life *(Matthew 5:48)*. We strive to do and be all that God wants us to be, knowing we'll fall short—and that applies to our gift giving this year as well. But by striving to have our gifts reflect God's gift to us—by keeping His gift in mind—we may be able to stay focused on giving instead of spending.

Giving like God gives. It's the way of Christmas.

Children

When I was growing up, most churches had some sort of a Christmas pageant every year. The average-size church could pull together enough grammar-school–age kids to be the cast and fill all the roles: shepherds, wise men, angels, the innkeeper, and the various animals that we assume were in the stable that eventful night. The plum roles, of course, were Mary and Joseph, given to a couple of the older, more dependable kids.

What a production! Shepherds in sandals and bathrobes with towels on their heads, multitudes of little angels in white choir robes with halos of gold tinsel positioned over their heads and gossamer wings pinned to their backs. I'm sure some adventuresome churches would use a real-life baby to play the part of Jesus, but most just laid a doll in the manger. The cutting-edge churches would run an extension cord to the manger with a lightbulb on the end to bathe the Jesus doll in a soft glow of light in the darkened sanctuary.

I read about one church that had the lightbulb-in-the-manger
arrangement—things were going well until someone offstage
tripped over the extension cord, unplugging it from the wall.
When the light in the manger went out, one of the shepherds, in
a much-too-loud whisper, looked in the direction of the cord and
hissed, *"Hey! You just unplugged Jesus!"*

It wouldn't be a Christmas pageant in church without a goof or two along those lines. And Christmas wouldn't be Christmas, either, without the innocence of children who seem to "get it" much more easily than we adults. They believe readily and they speak readily. They have no guile, no cynicism, no commercialization. If you tell a child that Christmas is when we celebrate Jesus' birthday, they're completely fine with that.

One family I read about had a tradition of setting an empty chair at their Christmas Day dinner to symbolize the presence of Jesus at their family's birthday celebration for Him. After all the presents had been opened on Christmas morning, the grandmother asked her little granddaughter, "Did you get everything you wanted for Christmas, dear?" And the little girl replied, "Well, no, but it's not really my birthday."

On the other hand, I heard about a small church that on its sign out front had the following message: "Remember Who is the reason for the season. Merry Christmas!" The pastor got a call from a lady in the community who was perturbed with the church's sign. The gist of her complaint was, "I just don't think the church ought to try to take over every holiday!"

Oh, the difference between children and adults at Christmas! I know, children aren't perfect. They sometimes manifest their carnal natures on Christmas morning—they're human, after all. But when it comes to the joy and innocence and celebratory part of Christmas that we adults so easily lose, children are our best examples. I believe every adult's Christmas would be better if they would spend those weeks thinking more like a child and less like an adult.

While this principle extends all year long, Christmas is one of the best times of the year to join with children in celebrating a heavenly Father who gives gifts so generously to His children. Not only did God the Father send God the Son into this world as the very first Christmas gift to His creation, He continues to give good gifts all year long as a manifestation of His generous grace. The apostle James calls them *"every good and every perfect gift"* (*James 1:17*). And Jesus Himself pointed out how God gives just what we need. When we ask for bread, He doesn't give a stone. When we ask for a fish He doesn't give a serpent. What father would do such a thing? Jesus said, *"If you then, being evil, know how to give good gifts to your children, how much more will your Father who is in heaven give good things to those who ask Him!"* (*Matthew 7:9–11*).

In spite of all the threats of "coal in your stocking," little children don't expect to get "bad" gifts from their parents. Our kids trust us!

They believe we have their best interests and their unadulterated joy in mind. Could there be a better opportunity than Christmas to convey to a child how much his heavenly Father loves him and that He has good gifts to give for a lifetime?

This Christmas, I encourage you to rekindle the wonder of Christmas that you may have had as a child. Be excited, be playful, be as extravagant as you can, and be a model of the excitement God has when He bestows gifts on us. And if you're feeling blue this Christmas, find a kid and brew up some hot chocolate—and you'll discover afresh why children are one of the ways of Christmas.

MUSIC

A group of Korean business leaders— all Christians—visited the United States recently with news about the plight of believers in North Korea. "There has been terrible persecution," they reported, "and thousands have died for their faith; yet many still worship despite danger and death threats. When they gather, it's in complete secrecy; and when they sing, it is done in silence. They open their mouths in unison, but they allow no sound from their voices for fear of being overheard." [II]

Imagine what it would be like to attend a Christmas Eve service this year and have to simply "mouth" the words of our great carols. Imagine being unable to hear the handbells, the chimes, the swelling crescendos of the "Hallelujah Chorus," or the pensive harmonies of "What Child Is This?"

What a privilege to sing the songs of Christmas! Yet we're so deluged by Christmas music each year that we're in danger of not hearing it at all. It's like the college student who highlighted every sentence of his textbook as the professor lectured from it in class. By the end of the semester, the whole book was highlighted—and as a result, nothing was highlighted. When we hear nonstop Christmas music in the elevators, in the malls, at church, on the radio, on the streets, and at home, we're in danger of its becoming mere background noise.

113

But carols are original elements of the nativity story, for the angelic choir composed and sang the first anthem: *"Glory to God in the highest, and on earth peace, goodwill toward men!" (Luke 2:14).* Have you ever paused to imagine what that sounded like? Myriad angels, a multitude of the heavenly host, lifting their voices in harmony, chanting or saying with all their hearts, the darkened skies strangely aglow with their luminous presence?

Every time we sing a Christmas carol, we're reenacting that wondrous scene.

I suggest you make a little purchase for yourself this month—a personal hymnbook or book of carols. Every Christian should keep a hymnal nearby. Older generations of believers thought of their hymnals as almost as precious as their Bibles, and they used them to round out their devotional time. Hymns emotionalize and personalize our doctrine and help our beliefs seep into our souls.

Learn to sing a hymn each day; and during this season, let it be a carol. Let your eyes linger over the words, and let the theology soak into your heart. I'm especially thrilled every time we get to verse two of Charles Wesley's "Hark, the Herald Angels Sing" because of that inspiring line saying, "Veiled in flesh the Godhead see; Hail th'incarnate Deity." That's a powerful affirmation that Jesus Christ, the Babe in the manger, was the eternal God Himself. He was "born to raise the sons of earth, born to give them second birth."

Web sites also list the words and music to thousands of hymns, many of which have fallen by the wayside in our popular church culture. Rediscovering them is one of the great joys of worship. Check out the German hymnist Paul Gerhardt, who wrote this powerful carol with its hauntingly beautiful melody. It should be rediscovered and sung in every church this season:

> *We sing, Immanuel, Thy praise,*
> *Thou Prince of Life and Fount of grace,*
> *Thou Flower of Heaven and Star of morn,*
> *Thou Lord of lords, Thou virgin born.*
> *Hallelujah!*

When you hear a carol at church or even in the store, pause and sing along, allowing your mind to focus on the words. Fill your home with the carols of Christmas. In so doing, you can enjoy spontaneous moments of worship throughout the day.

It's one of the ways of Christmas.

117

TRADITION

The great innovator Henry Ford cared little for the past. His famous saying was, "History is bunk." But, as Stephen J. Nichols points out in his book *The Reformation*, history has always been crucial to the people of God. In the Bible, the writers continually told God's people to *remember*. For them, it wasn't "Remember the Alamo," but "Remember the Exodus" in the Old Testament and "Remember the Resurrection" in the New.

"When something significant occurred in the life of Israel," Nichols points out, "they erected a monument so they and future generations would remember what great things God had done for them." [12]

The apostle Peter told his readers that his letter wasn't intended to present new ideas, but *"to remind you always of these things, though you know and are established in [them] . . . to stir you up by reminding you"* (2 Peter 1:12–13).

Traditions are habits that remind us of God's past faithfulness. They are patterns that preserve precious links between our past and our future, events through which the heritage of our forefathers is instilled within the hearts of our children.

When it comes to Christmas, there are two kinds of traditions, and both are important.

COMMON TRADITIONS

Common traditions are those that are shared by many people in a society, such as gift giving, Christmas trees, and holiday music. Many traditions go back many centuries. You might be surprised to learn that one of the oldest Christmas traditions is hanging stockings on the chimney. It dates from the days of Pastor Nicholas, the much-loved bishop of Myra in the fourth century.

In one of his ministry trips, Pastor Nicholas was reportedly visiting in a particular city when he heard of an impoverished widower who had no money for his daughter's dowry. Wanting to provide anonymously for this family, Nicholas went to the home by night, reached through the window, and tossed a small bag of coins into the stocking drying by the fireplace.

His deed was eventually found out; and after Nicholas died, a day was set apart in the church calendar to commemorate his life. It became a custom for children to hang their stockings by the fireplace on St. Nicholas Day. During the night, a useful treat would be placed in the stocking; and the next morning, the children would awaken and run to their stocking to discover what was there.

Most of our Christmas traditions have interesting historical roots like that, and they can be useful teaching opportunities for families with children.

PERSONAL TRADITIONS

Even better, however, are our own personal traditions—those that are unique to our families. In her book *Our Christmas Story*, Mrs. Billy Graham wrote, "My mother always served oyster stew for Christmas breakfast when I was a girl in China. It was a family custom." As a mother herself, Mrs. Graham continued the tradition, although she said she had to explain every year to the man at the grocery store why she was looking for fresh oysters on Christmas Eve.

Every family needs its own traditions, and the great thing about traditions is that you can start one anytime. It might be reading the Christmas story around the tree, enjoying a snow picnic on the back porch, or devoting Christmas morning to serving in a homeless shelter. Perhaps a special menu (it doesn't have to be oyster stew), a yearly trip (even if it's just driving around town looking at the lights), or a different approach to gift giving. Some traditions are old-fashioned and others are wacky, but all of them build memories and preserve the heritage of our values and families.

This year, enjoy the traditions of Christmas, use them to full advantage for your family, and maybe even begin a new one of your own.

That's one of the ways of Christmas.

127

Endnotes

1 O.Henry. The Four Million. (New York: A.L. Burt Co, 1906), 25.

2 Henry Ward Beecher. Life Thoughts. (Edinburgh: Alexander Strahan, 1858),13

3 F.B. Meyer. Steps into the Blessed Life. (Philadelphia, PA: Altemus, 1896)

4 Mother Teresa. Nobel Peace Prize acceptance speech. December 10, 1979.

5 "Brave Jake to Turn On Christmas Lights. North-West Evening Mail. November 22, 2006. At:www.nwemail.co.uk.

6 Neiman Marcus 2007 Fantasy Gifts.

7 Dick Francis, Under Orders. (New York: Putnam, 2006), 74.

8 Quoted in Thomas A. Spragens, Civil Liberalism: Reflections on our Democratic Ideals (Lanham, MD: Rowman and Littlefield Publishers, Inc., 1999), 189.

9 www.christianitytoday.com/ct/2006/december/29.54.html.

10 www.nrf.com/modules.php?name=Document&op=viewlive&sp_id=61.

11 Robert J. Morgan, Come Let Us Adore Him: Stories Behind the Most Cherished Christmas Hymns (Thomas Nelson, 2005), 6.

12 Stephen J. Nichols, The Reformation: How a Monk and a Mallet Changed the World (Wheaton: Crossway Books, 2007), 13.